Émerson Felipe Neves dos Santos
Jeffson Verissimo de Oliveira

REVERSE LOGISTICS, SUSTAINABILITY AND SOCIAL ENTREPRENEURSHIP

Émerson Felipe Neves dos Santos
Jeffson Verissimo de Oliveira

REVERSE LOGISTICS, SUSTAINABILITY AND SOCIAL ENTREPRENEURSHIP

ACHIEVING SUCCESS IN SOCIAL PROJECTS

ScienciaScripts

May your efforts defy the impossibilities, remember that the great things of man have been conquered from what seemed impossible.

(Charles Chaplin)

SUMMARY

Today natural resources are increasingly scarce due to predatory exploitation of man, it is important to direct studies on reverse logistics aimed at sustainability that is essential for human survival, but especially for future generations. Therefore, projects that encompass this area have great value. And, with this alignment, focused on social entrepreneurship can contribute to a better quality of life for people who will be included in this environment. This work aims to demonstrate through social entrepreneurship how the process of recycling fish scales works using reverse logistics, in an association of artisans, COPESCA, located in the city of CAMALAÚ-PB, through sustainable actions, where it recycles and uses scales to make craft pieces favoring the municipal sustainability. For this, an interview granted by the president of the colony was carried out for the collection of data in addition to *on-site visits* and direct observation. Thus, with the results, it was verified that through social entrepreneurship it is possible to transform and develop a certain region through sustainable practices such as reverse logistics and offer a better quality of life to those residents belonging to COPESCA. In the economic dimension it provided an extra income to the family of the members and it was possible to delimit the expenses of the manufactured products and the selling price of each product, in the social dimension it promoted the social inclusion of these women and finally, in the environmental dimension it reused the organic residues (scales) that would be discarded in the environment, thus providing great benefit to sustainable development. Thus, it is concluded that through the dimensions of sustainability, social enterprises can be an alternative for humble communities without much prospect of improving the quality of life.

Keywords: Reverse Logistics. Social Entrepreneurship. Sustainability Triad.

ABSTRACT

In the now day world that natural resources are each time more scarce due to the predatory exploration from the human being, so it is important to promote studies referent to the reverse logistics aiming the sustainability which is essential to the actual human generation, more primary for the future generations, then, projects involving this area has great value. In addition, aligned to this ideal initiative, for the social entrepreneurship can contribute to a better quality of life of people that are included in this environment. Being so, this paper has as goal demonstrate onwards the social entrepreneurship how works the recycling process of fish's scales using reverse logistics, in one artisans' association, the COPESCA, situated at the city of CAMALAU-PB, through sustainable actions where they recycle and use scales for manufacturing artisanal pieces in favor of city's sustainability. For that was made an interview with the colony's president for gather some data and visits *in loco* for direct observation. Thereby, in the results, it was verified that through social entrepreneurship is possible to transform and develop certain regions through sustainable practices like reverse logistics offering a better quality of life to those who belongs to the COPESCA. In the economical dimension provides some extra money to the associated families and was also possible to delimit costs of manufactured products and the selling prices of each product, in the social dimension, was promoted the social inclusion of the women and finally, in the environmental dimension, was recycled organic wastes (scales) that would be discarded in the environment, promoting, great benefits for sustainable development. Like that, was concluded that through the sustainable dimensions, social entrepreneurship can be an alternative for poor communities with no expectations for a better life.

Keywords : Reverse logistics. Social Entrepreneurship. Triad of Sustainability.

LIST OF ABBREVIATIONS

IBGE - Brazilian Institute of Geography Statistics

COPESCA - Fishermen's Colony

CVP - Product Life **Cycle**

NGO - Non Governmental Organization

SEBRAE - Brazilian Support Service for Micro and Small Businesses

1INTRODUCTION

With the growing world population, fundamental needs arise for the survival of the current generation and also the conservation of resources for future generations. Aiming at this, sustainable development was created trying to use maneuvers that encompass the whole society with a common good, making strategies that reduce environmental pollution and save the maximum resources available in nature.

It can be noted that the definition of sustainable development is being very widespread, "sustainable development is therefore characterized not as a fixed state of harmony, but as a process of change in which the exploitation of resources, the management of technological investment and institutional changes are made compatible with the present and the future". (CANEPA, 2007). As a result, the population is increasingly concerned about the various aspects that go against the ecological balance.

An area intrinsically related to sustainable development is reverse logistics, which uses reverse distribution channels, causing materials that would be dumped into the environment to cause pollution, thus having a prolonged life cycle (post-consumption), or turning into new products, through recycling, reuse or proper disposal.

These new products offer the association the opportunity to profit and develop a social role in the community, since people who have few opportunities in the labor market are inserted. It is a new business model that has been spreading in the world, social entrepreneurship, whose hallmark is the idea that, through innovative solutions, they can solve social problems.

In the case of social entrepreneurship, this research has as object of study the cooperative of fishermen of the city of Camalaú Paraíba, which through aquaculture, which is based on the cultivation of fish for a better quality of the product, that the association can obtain greater bargaining power in front of a market that every day is more competitive.

With this approach it is possible to remove organic waste from the environment, thus contributing to sustainability, insert people in social projects generating more opportunities, and also provide extra income to low-income families. All these aspects seen show the importance of social entrepreneurship with the quality of life of people who are included in this environment, qualities that in addition to providing income and social insertion, educates the agents involved to a world where people care about nature, worry about not wasting things that can be reused.

So, how can social entrepreneurship contribute to improving the quality of life in an association of artisans - COPESCA using reverse logistics through sustainability?

This study aims to demonstrate a social enterprise in the process of recycling fish scales using reverse logistics in a sustainable way in an association of artisans located in the city of CAMALAÚ-PB.

1.1 OBJECTIVES

1.1.1 General

- To demonstrate how social entrepreneurship through reverse logistics with a focus on sustainability contributes to the fishermen colony - "COPESCA" in the municipality of Camalaú-PB.

1.1.2 Specific

- Search for bibliographic concepts regarding social entrepreneurship, reverse logistics and sustainability;
- Identify how social entrepreneurship is present in COPESCA;
- Describe the reverse logistics in the fish scale processing process;
- Present the impact of sustainability at COPESCA for women members and the community.
- To point out the contribution of social entrepreneurship to reverse logistics at COPESCA through sustainable actions.
- Present the financial gains of each artisanal product sold.

1.2 STRUCTURE OF WORK

The present work is composed of five chapters. The first chapter shows the introduction, which defines the theme and the problems of the research, the justification, objectives and the structural part of the work.

The second chapter presents the theoretical foundations of the research, pondering on social entrepreneurship, fish farming, business logistics and reverse logistics, product life cycle, crafts as reverse logistics, sustainability, organic solid waste.

The third chapter is the scientific methodology part of the work.

Chapter four sets out the results of the survey, in which all reverse logistical methods are applied for good reuse of inputs.

Finally, chapter five presents the final considerations of the survey.

2 THEORETICAL BACKGROUND

In this chapter, the main concepts and definitions that served as a basis for the development of this work will be discussed, showing the concepts and objectives of social entrepreneurship, fish farming, business logistics and reverse logistics, product life cycle, crafts as reverse logistics, sustainability, organic solid waste.

2.1 SOCIAL ENTREPRENEURSHIP

Being an entrepreneur is seen as a person with a broad vision on a certain subject, who is not afraid to break the routine, to be radical in his conceptions and to take risks, provided that the risks are well evaluated. The scenario for an entrepreneur is full of options to take action and solve the problems, these measures are innovative, creative and with cheaper costs with higher income possibilities. For Dornelas (2008) entrepreneur is the one who finds a chance and creates a business to profit from it, taking previously calculated risks.

Entrepreneurship for Dolabela (2010) corresponds to a process of converting dreams into reality and heritage. And Dornelas (2008) also addresses that entrepreneurship is the involvement of individuals and processes that together lead to the transformation of concepts into opportunities.

Social entrepreneurship, although considered a new theme, some authors report that it already existed, even with other denominations. Oliveira (2004, p.10) reports that "The theme of social entrepreneurship is new in its current configuration, but in its essence it has existed for a long time. Some experts point out Luther King, Gandhi, among others, as social entrepreneurs. This was a result of his leadership and innovation abilities regarding large scale changes".

Oliveira (2004, p.12) addresses what is not social entrepreneurship, according to his experience.

> Social entrepreneurship is not a corporate social responsibility, as it implies an organized and properly planned set of internal and external actions, and a definition centered on the company's mission and activity, in view of the community's needs. It is not a profession, since it is not legally constituted, there is no university or technical education, no regulatory council and no legal code of professional ethics; it is also not a social organization that produces and generates revenues from the sale of products and services, much less is represented by an entrepreneur who invests in the social field, which is closer to corporate social responsibility, or at most, philanthropy and corporate charity".

After addressing what is not social entrepreneurship, Vale (2004) says that the social entrepreneur is that person, whose primary function is to improve processes together, generating greater competitiveness and economic development.

According to Melo Neto and Froes (2002, p.34), "not just anyone can be a social entrepreneur. Social entrepreneurship is a mixture of science and art, rationality and intuition, idea and vision, social sensitivity and responsible pragmatism, utopia and reality, innovative strength and practicality".

It is important to remember that social entrepreneurs are different from traditional entrepreneurs, who take risks for their own benefit or for the benefit of the organization, the key characteristic of social entrepreneurs is that they take risks for the benefit of the people their organization serves (BRINCKERHOFF, 2000, p.1).

And, social entrepreneurship at COPESCA takes shape for its use through inputs from fish farming, showing the interaction between the parties in order to solve the problems of wasted inputs.

2.2 FISH FARMING

Fish farming is one of the areas of study of aquaculture, which is based on fish farming. According to VALENTI (2000), aquaculture in Brazil shows six main areas determined by the groups of organisms farmed: freshwater fish, sea shrimps, mussels, oysters, freshwater shrimps and frogs.

In Brazil one of the areas that has been gaining more space is fish farming, because the country has a great capacity for evolution, its climate helps in development. The activity has increased markedly because profitability has good prospects, and provides a rapid return on the capital invested by the rural producer (OSTRENSKY and BOEGER, 1998).
According to BARBOSA (1992), there are many benefits of fish farming: it can use unproductive areas for agriculture and livestock, it can develop easily on some land (salty and flooded), the investment has a rapid return, you can have a high productivity per area and also the fact that fish live in liquid environment and are cold-blooded animals are positive factors.

There is a concern for care in both fish farming activities and aquaculture in general, as it needs care for ecosystems. This is why the "Code of Conduct for Responsible Fisheries" (FAO, 1995) was created. This code comes as a way to further help maintain sustainable standards in activities, and one way to ensure this is through reverse logistics, as it ensures that products are discarded in the environment and return to become new products, thus reducing various environmental problems.

2.3 BUSINESS LOGISTICS AND REVERSE LOGISTICS

According to Hong (1999), the logistical definition, has been in the forefront since the 1940s, the US armed forces used this area. It interacted with the entire process of acquiring and supplying materials in World War II, used by the U.S. military to meet all the combat objectives of the time.

Logistics, a traditional area of administration and an essential stage in many industrial and commercial activities, is responsible for the product's journey from the acquisition of the raw material to the point of final consumption. Thus, the logistics activity includes the establishment of relations between manufacturers and retailers, in addition to the delivery of goods to consumers. The components of a normal logistics system are: customer service, demand forecasting, distribution communications, inventory control, material handling, order processing, spare parts and support services, choice of factory locations, packaging, handling of returned products, scrap recycling, traffic and transportation, storage and warehousing (BALLOU, 2006).

One of the areas of logistics is reverse logistics, according to (REVLOG, 2005, CHAVES and BATALHA, 2006) is a vast activity that encompasses all operations related to the reuse of products and materials such as the logistics activities of collection, disassembly and process of products and/or materials and parts used to ensure their sustainable recovery and that does not damage the environment. In order to have a reverse flow, there is a set of activities that a company can perform or outsource. These include the collection, separation, packaging and shipment of used, damaged or obsolete items from the point of sale (or consumption) to those of reprocessing, recycling, resale or disposal (Steven, 2004, CHAVES and BATALHA, 2006).

According to Leite (2003) reverse logistics can be classified according to the type of return in post-consumption and post-sales items. Both following the reverse channel of traditional direct distribution of goods. These reverse distribution channels address a portion of products with little use after sale, with extended life cycle or after extinction of their useful life, return to the productive or business cycle, regaining value in secondary markets by reuse or recycling of their constituent materials.

Figure 1: Direct and reverse distribution channels.

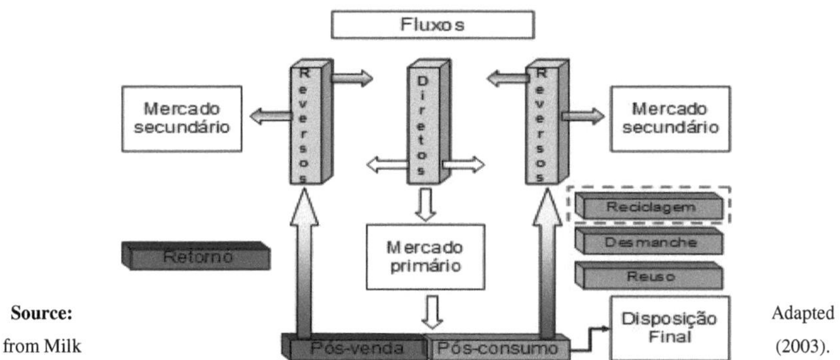

Source: from Milk

Adapted (2003).

Leite (2003) says that the distribution of reverse channels of post-consumer goods are in three specifications, having as prerequisite durable or semi-durable goods. It can be presented as the reverse channels of reuse, dismantling or recycling, characterized by the lengthening of the useful life of the product, adding value to it. In the non-reuse of these products within the reverse logistics, it is destined for final disposal, having these products their final stage.

In this study, the product in question is classified as a post-consumption good, presenting itself, due to its characteristics in the reverse channels, as a recycling product. Leite (2003) addresses the reverse channel of recycling, in which materials from the rejected inputs are transformed into secondary or recycled raw materials that will be included in the manufacture of new products, going through gradual steps of collection, selection, preparation, recycling and reintegration into the production cycle.

2.4 PRODUCT LIFE CYCLE

For Freire (2010) every day the products are more practical, in ever smaller portions and with lower shelf life and this is caused by the use of more primary and secondary packaging and with large and increasingly active *marketing* incentives, which use new media processes, to encourage consumption, and consequently, greater waste disposal.

According to Kotler (2006), an input is considered to be some element that has the function of meeting a particular need of a consumer. Where, Irigaray *et al.* (2006), says that a product can be anything tangible (a product, for example) or intangible (a service).

According to Lamb Jr. *et al.* (2004, p. 337) "The life cycle of a product provides a way to control the stages of acceptance of a product, from its release (birth) to its decline. In which the Product Life Cycle (PVC) is divided into four stages: Introduction, Growth, Maturity and Decline, according to figure 2:

Figure 2 - Product Life **Cycle**

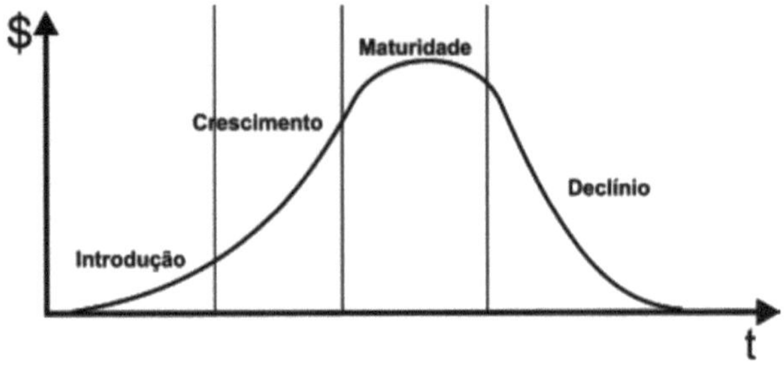

Source: Kotler and Armstrong (2003, p.251).

For Corbari and Macedo (2012), the cycle involves from the initial period of the product to the final stage of its economic exploitation and is comprised of four stages:

Introduction: this is the period of little growth in sales and a high production cost. It is the launch period, so strong investments in *marketing*, technology and distribution are required.

Growth: Moment at which there is greater acceptance by customers and financial return is increasing. Best sales phase of the product.

Maturity: period in which there is a low growth in sales, profits decrease or tend to be stabilized due to the increase of competitors.

Decline: This is the stage where sales and profits fall. It is the time to analyze if the product will leave the market or if there will be a process of innovation.

According to Lacerda (2009), when analyzing from the perspective of logistics, a product does not have the end of its life cycle when it is delivered to the customer, because they can return to their origin due to disposal, repair or reuse, which directly influences the costs.

In order to prolong the life cycle of a product, the design of the use of components that would be treated as something 'unused', can be used, and become the main parts of a new product, with artisanal characteristics, which is the case of fish scales. Where artisans, creatively, manage to give value to what would be garbage.

2.5 CRAFTS AS REVERSE LOGISTICS

According to FOUCAULT (2002) craftsmanship is seen as a practice that comes from a cultural dynamic, and not as a static and/or palpable object, sometimes seen with a certain "naturalness".

Handicraft is present in all known cultures and is important for understanding the history of each society. According to Soto (2003, p. 36) the production of handicraft is an expression deeply linked to popular culture, because it is a response to the needs of a society, a people or a certain region and eternalizes the typical traits of the culture that generates it. Jongerward (2002) also addresses that classical methods and various forms of crafts reflect millennia of cultural suitability and changes that occur at the interface between cultures, generations and individuals.

Reverse logistics is linked to the contribution to the environment, in order to find solutions to stop the discarded inputs. And Novaes (2007, p. 53) addresses that "Reverse Logistics takes care of material flows that start at the points of consumption of products and end at the points of origin, with the aim of recovering value or final disposal. And an intelligent solution found to use these discarded materials is craftsmanship, in which Kazazian (2005) points out that using discarded materials is one of the propositions of eco design, which by assessing the life cycle of the product, adding function to the materials, which become an input in a new process, reduces environmental impacts.

For Silva (2009, p. 4)

> Craftsmanship considers the four dimensions proposed by sustainability: social, by generating work and income for economically disadvantaged people; environmental, by enabling the use of waste discarded early and less harmful materials; economic, by being directed for marketing purposes based on the identification of a demand; and cultural, by respecting the individuality of the artisan and the local characteristics of the community to which he belongs and preserving the local culture.

Linking craftsmanship as reverse logistics with a focus on sustainability becomes a dimension of unparalleled importance from the point of view beneficial to sustainable development, as it has a whole philosophy of care for the environment, especially when the product used by craftsmen uses raw material for recycling.

2.6 SUSTAINABILITY

Sustainability is exposed as the management and administration of resources/services, as well as the guide to technological and institutional changes, seeking to ensure and reach a constant supply of human needs for present and future generations, taking into account the limits of the sustaining capacity of environmental systems (RODRIGUEZ, 2001).

By rediscovering the notion of the finitude of natural resources, society puts in check the predatory behavior of the human being in the process of occupation and civilization of geographical space. If, on the one hand, this rediscovery inserts as a fundamental premise the "sustainability" of man's economic and social behavior, on the other hand, it comes from measures of control and ordering of human behavior, with the aim of preventing ecological and environmental crisis of unknown dimensions. (MILANI, 1999b).

Figure 3 addresses the premises of the triad of sustainability, in the economic, environmental and social responsibility spheres:

Figure 3 - Triad of sustainability.

Source: Brundtland Report (1987).

For Camino and Muller (1993), sustainability has multiple dimensions and should be complementary: social justice, economic viability, environmental sustainability, democracy, solidarity and ethics. The importance given to certain dimensions depends on the objectives and the context in which the studies are conducted.

For Santos, Barbosa and Carvalho (2013), the definition of sustainable development appears to be very convincing and very efficient in theory, but its application in general and addressing environmental, technological, economic, cultural and political issues, shows to be complicated, because the behaviors in the act of acting, thinking, producing and consuming of humanity changes, as well as the participation of all areas of society to implement these changes.

2.7 ORGANIC SOLID WASTE

Organic waste is waste from animals and plants, which is no longer used but discarded to pollute the environment. But, like other types of waste, they can be reused, reducing landfills and dumps. Their reuse in waste sorting centers and/or organic matter composting can generate reusable substances, such as organic fertilizer, among others. What occurs, however, is that organic waste is not separated from other waste, being contaminated by various toxic materials, losing its capacity to be reused, which makes it of fundamental importance to prevent and correctly separate domestic waste before its collection and final destination.

Another attribute that makes previous separation of organic waste essential is that it comes from the slurry present in dumps and landfills. In this design, the reduction of organic waste would reduce the occurrence of such a polluting substance to the environment (IBGE, 2010).

This type of waste is analysed as a pollutant and, when agglomerated, it can become highly unattractive and have a bad smell, usually due to the decomposition of these products. If no basic care is taken with the storage of waste, the environment is conducive to the development of micro-organisms that are often agents and cause disease. Organic waste can be decomposed (NETO, et al., 2007).

Organic waste is a major problem, because a small percentage of its use can be adapted to post-consumption, due to its short life cycle and invalidation for consumption, so this waste has its final disposal, either in landfills or dumps, in a very short time. In this way, adverse solutions that can undermine the disposal of these wastes are of utmost importance.

3METODOLOGY

The study is defined as research, where Minayo (1993) addresses that research is the essential activity of the sciences in their questioning and discovery of reality. It is requested when there is no satisfactory information about the answer to the problem or when the exposed information is not in accordance with it. Demo (1996) includes research as a regular activity, considering it as a form of measures whose function is to seek answers to proposed questions based on rational and systematic procedures.

As for the nature of this research, it is classified as an Applied Research, because, according to Collis and Hussey (2005, p.27), "it was designed to apply its findings to a specific existing problem". Applied research has the function of resulting knowledge for the good use of practices aimed at solutions of particular problems, including local truths and interests. Gil (2010, p.27) highlights that applied research is "research aimed at acquiring knowledge for application in a specific situation". With this, this study distinguishes itself as an applied research, as it made use of the existing theory on social entrepreneurship, reverse logistics and sustainability, conducting its application in a fishermen's cooperative located in the Paraiba Cariri region.

The approach to the problem is based on qualitative elements, because according to Silva and Menezes (2001), it shows that there is an effective similarity between the real world and the subject, and it cannot be reported in numbers, and the study of the data is done inductively. Bogdan & Biklen (2003), show that the definition of qualitative research relates five main characteristics that conform this type of study: natural environment, descriptive data, concern with the process, concern with the meaning and process of inductive analysis. This is identified by examining the facts and relating them from data analysis so that activities are understood in a subjective manner.

Regarding the objectives, the research is characterized as descriptive, which according to Vergara (2000) shows characteristics of a certain population or of a certain fact, but has no obligation to clarify the facts it describes, although it is the basis for such explanation. It can establish connections between all the variables and determine their nature. The research presented here is descriptive, since it analyzes all the process variables for certain studies concerning social entrepreneurship, reverse logistics and sustainability. It is classified as exploratory because, according to Gil (1991, p.45), it seeks to provide greater familiarity with the problem, with the intention of making it explicit or building theories, having as its main function the improvement of ideas or the discovery of intuitions. For Zikmund (2000), exploratory studies are generally favorable for diagnosing cases, exploring alternatives or discovering new ideas. In this sense, we have tried to clarify and define the nature of the problem which is precisely the waste of inputs, especially scales, and have tried to add value with this problem.

According to the technical procedures, bibliographical research is constituted. According to Vergara (2000), the bibliographic research is developed from material already formed, consisting especially of scientific books and articles and has importance for the survey of fundamental data on direct and indirect aspects related to the subject.

In the research there was a survey of the bibliography in published materials, such as scientific articles, web pages, books, etc. This research is also labeled as a survey, because Gil (2010) states that it occurs when it involves the direct questioning of people in which attitudes are studied in order to get to know each other. All the information was acquired during visits at COPESCA.

It is also characterized as a case study, in which Yin (2001), exposes as an intense and pulled study of the events subject to verification, allowing a wide and detailed knowledge of the real and the facts analyzed. Severino (2007, p. 121) also demonstrates that "it concentrates on the study of a particular case, considered to be representative of a set of analogous cases, by him significantly representative". In the study, it sought to precisely analyze all the parameters relating to social entrepreneurship, reverse logistics and sustainability in order to have a significant deepening on the explicit content.

The period in which the studies were carried out was from June to October 2015, which through an in-depth search of bibliographic references, sought to develop a more compact and accurate research for a better result regarding what was proposed in the theme.

Means were used to record all the contents, such as camera, mobile phone, computer, in order to have a holistic view of the whole study site and thus be able to analyze important issues that would enable their solution.

For data collection, several semi-structured interviews were conducted which, according to Triviños (1987, p.146) is the key point of trivial questioning based on theories and hypotheses that have to do with the research theme. And were granted by the president of the colony in the months of June to October 2015, where information was obtained regarding the social entrepreneurship present, about the process of recycling scales, which is where is included the whole reverse logistic process and the importance for sustainability, not counting the sight *in loco* weekly in the periods of manufacture of products.

4RESULTS

4.1 CASE STUDY: IDENTIFICATION OF THE COMPANY

COPESCA is a fishing colony located in the city of Camalaú in the Paraibano cariri, it has about 70 (seventy) associates, among these, only 5 (five) women participate in the group that do the process of recycling the scale, as well as the assembly of products sold by the association itself. The association has already been awarded, having as representative/president Mrs. Maria de Fátimaqueinovou a process of shredding the fish "traíra" erecebe the gold prize of SEBRAE in the category rural producer in the year 2013 at state level and, later national, which caused trips to European countries (Sweden and Norway) to meet companies of fish processing. In July 2014 this small group of the association started to produce using recycled scales, which became the main component of products made by hand. The artisans specialized with a fish scale recycling course provided by CUNHÃ, which is an NGO (Non Governmental Organization) supporting the work of women in the Caribbean Paraiba.

Image 1 and Aquaculture2 (COPESCA).

Source:own authorship (2015)

Image 1 shows the front of the fishing colony, where the members also work with the scales.

4.2 COPESCA AND SOCIAL ENTREPRENEURSHIP

Innovation has always been a parameter of great relevance at COPESCA, from the unique model of improvement of the shredding of the traitor fish, which was studied in the kitchen of the house of the president, Mrs. Maria de Fátima and which generated an award to her and to the association, to the new products that are included in the cooperative, the articles from the scales. And it is these that bring out social entrepreneurship and how important it is for the local scene.

The idea of "scale art" also came from Mrs. Maria de Fátima, who noticed the possibility of recycling scales through products to sell. But the main reason was not only the possibility of making a profit, but the insertion of the fishermen's wives in the cooperative, who were seen as housewives, without opportunities or any other profession and who were now part of a totally different scenario, which allowed them great learning, extra money for their homes, and most importantly, the opportunity to be inserted in a social group linked to sustainability.

In an interview with the President of the cooperative, she was asked if she already felt like a professional in scale craftsmanship. In response, she approached:

> "Honestly, I am Fatima I am not an artisan who considers herself a professional, but I give all my support so that the artisans here in Camalaú develop the most beautiful work possible, like the fishermen of Sumé and Congo. That at the peak of fishing production, they can take advantage of this material and make the most beautiful arrangements and the most beautiful bouquets".

In view of the interviewee's speech, it is clear that there is a concern to pass on the knowledge acquired from making handicrafts to other municipalities and with this provide a better quality of life for other families through the marketing of recycled products.

She was asked if there were any associates who were already a reference, she spoke:

> "Here in Camalaú I stand out as an artisan who can take with great art Ivanilde, because she both does and teaches for others and encourages production, because if we sell any piece to a person from far away, we are sending the name of the city and the name of the fishermen of the region.

She then spoke about the importance of preserving this culture of recycling:

> "So we want to make sure that the art in the fish scale here in the cariri doesn't die, it's a dedicated job, because our scale is small, but we have to work with the wealth that we have".

Thus, the presence of reverse logistics in the face of sustainable actions is notorious, thus favoring social entrepreneurship, where the recycling of fish scales through its processing favors sustainable actions for the region.

Then, as she is a woman of great vision, she has already talked about new perspectives of taking advantage of other regional inputs along with scales:

> "We also want to add the seeds of the region, the wood, the bark as a form of dyeing the scales. We want to add these products to the scale so that they are sustainable products and that the other product that is being natively discarded there in the field is used as a resource wealth for survival, because we are women, but we know how to value the products we have, right? So, what is waste we are already seeing with another face, with the eyes of sustainability and that gives quality of life and good looks to the municipalities of Camalaú. That's what I wish!".

It is important to observe the environmental concern not only with the inputs of the colony, but also with others that are in different systems, being able to unite in a common good, and add even more people to be benefited with projects of this character.

Faced with the above definitions, COPESCA, a fishermen's colony in the city of Camalaú - PB, based on the customization of the scales coming from fish, shows to follow in a very explicit way the parameters of social entrepreneurship, because it managed to innovate its products with the recycling of scales, in addition to benefiting several associated by offering the opportunity to produce with the inputs that would be thrown into the environment, bringing them to a scenario of socialization, in addition to adding the financial factor for their families and showing the sustainability factor in focus.

4.3 SUSTAINABILITY ANALYSIS

The analysis is based on the triad of sustainability, which shows the positive points in environmental, social and economic terms.

The collection of organic waste brings innumerable benefits to the environment, since it remains on the banks of the dams causing bad smell, infertility to the soil and accumulation of garbage, in addition to compromising water quality. In the case of the fishermen of COPESCA, there is a great accumulation of garbage, because the cleaning of the fish (removal of the scales, head, tail and viscera) is done on the bank of the dam, causing all these evils. Therefore, the removal of these debris will make possible the conservation of the entire area that the fishermen work on, improving the vision of the place, reducing the presence of insects and especially reducing the emission of garbage thrown into the environment. To be able to remove from the environment in a precise way, the associated companies must first do a work to raise awareness among fishermen, because they don't have access to this type of information and end up contributing to environmental pollution. Then, just like the fish that went through the cleaning process, the waste that was once thrown into the environment will now also be taken away in the same way only in different compartments (buckets identified by name and color according to inputs) so that the colony can take the proper use. And now, the waste will have a new direction and new processes, further reducing environmental pollution.

In the social field, this project has great value because it offers those associated with the opportunity to improve the quality of their lives and their families, resulting in people with a high cultural and educational level, a sharper look at sustainable practices, and a group of people who had few opportunities in the community and would now be included in a project of great relevance, thus generating much motivation, well being, pride forever continue and call more people. This affects both the community present and elsewhere, as these people will be an example and reference for more people to be included in this project or inspire other possibilities for plans in this direction.

Considering the economic part of the triad of sustainability, the project of the referred study has a great contribution for the people who participate in it, because they are of low income and this extra income   is of paramount importance for the families of the artisans, because it provides opportunities to supply other needs of their homes.

Box 1 shows the sustainable prospects of the colony in the three dimensions: economic, environmental and social:

Table 1 - Sustainable **perspectives**.

	Sustainable Perspectives
Economic dimension	Decrease in raw material costs; Increase sales; Partnership with suppliers of inputs needed for production. A marketing focused on sustainability; Acquisition of new equipment.
Environmental dimension	Follow the standard of waste control; Increase recycling of inputs; Awareness of fishermen; Transportation of inputs in specific containers; Improve the entire area of activity of

	fishermen.
Social dimension	To accompany and guide the members; To encourage members in sustainable practices; To insert more people into the cooperative; To be a reference for the community and region.

Source: Own authorship (2016).

In the economic dimension what is expected from the sustainable perspectives is that there will be a considerable reduction in the costs with raw material from the fish waste itself and also by buying the necessary inputs in larger quantities so that the price is more taken into account and to achieve greater bargaining power with suppliers through partnerships. With the focus also to increase gains through this reduction in costs and thus improve sales, which can be from a greater marketing to sell more products, the inclusion of articles in stores of artisanal products, in exhibitions at congresses that focus on sustainable products, among others. It can be of help so that in the future the income can increase even more and thus the colony improves all its infrastructure, from the size of its area, to the comfort of its accommodations. It is also intended to acquire more technological equipment to facilitate the development of the members' work.

The environmental dimension, in order to continue in a very sustainable way, must follow the standard of waste control, according to the Brazilian norms that deal with this particular subject, through congresses and lectures for the fishermen to become aware and begin to follow this culture, and for them to initiate interventions to remove, in a conscious and specific way, the waste that is in the field of work, causing in future actions, a satisfactory improvement of the whole area of action of the fishermen and thus, the growth in the number of products recycled through the maintenance of a cycle of continuous improvement in the reuse of inputs.

In the social dimension it is important to have the accompaniment of the president and the most experienced members to guide the new members to the above mentioned practices and to show the importance of each one to the contribution of social development and thus to offer opportunities to the members and incentives to sustainable practices, developing new forms of inclusion that attract more people with the same line of thought, thus being able to be a reference in the whole region.

4.4 FISH SCALE RECYCLING PROCESS

In Figure 5 we can see how the fish scale recycling process works, where all the steps are addressed so that the recycling can be satisfactorily completed.

Figure 4 - Fish scale recycling **process.**

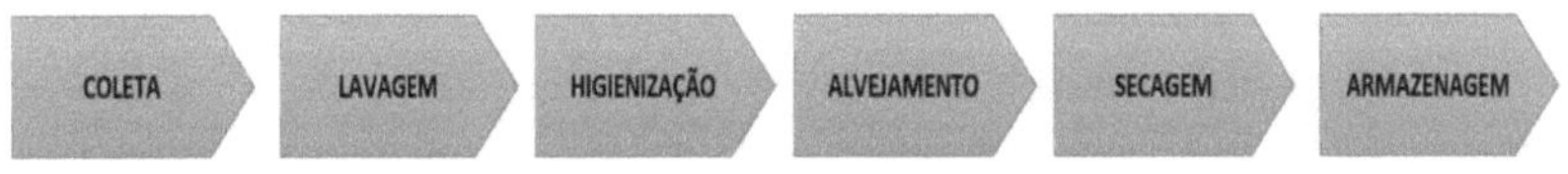

Source: own authorship (2015).

In the logical sequence, all steps of the required process will be classified:

First step (collection): In the collection the group disposed of the recycling gets scales that will be treated, with other associates that fish to sell in form of fish file, in this format only the parts where the fish have meat without bones are used. Soon, the rest was thrown away, in this case the other parts of the fish ended up being dumped inside the dam itself that were caught or left on the edge of it.

The collection of the scales is done by the members themselves who participate in the process, who search the houses of the association's fishermen, in which some make the separation of the scales from other waste not used by the fish for them, in other cases the members themselves need to make this separation. Some fishermen leave them directly at the association's site, but in all cases they make the selection of what will be used in the recycling process.

Second step (washing): This procedure starts with the division of the 3 (three) different types of scales, which will be according to the species of fish, which are: tilapia, traitor and curimatan. These scales cannot be mixed in any way, because each type has a specific density, that if mixed in the wash they get embolished, become brittle and end up losing quality. After that it starts to be washed with water, to remove dirt from the scales, such as earth and small pieces of stones that stay together. Several washes are necessary so that it starts to get a more satisfactory color tone. And the number of washes varies, because it depends a lot on the state of dirt of the scales and also the experience of the associates in doing this operation.

Third step (sanitization): After washing, the scales are submerged in buckets containing water mixed with bleach, in the proportion that for each liter of water is ideal approximately 4 (four) to 5 (five) spoons of bleach, for about 2 (two) or 3 (three) hours, thus losing the bad smell of fish. After this time in the buckets, the scales are removed and washed again in running water, removing the bleach.

Fourth step (bleaching): In this step the scales are deposited in containers containing a bleach without the chlorine, leaving them soft and smelly.

Fifth step (drying): **Drying** should be done in a covered place, without exposure to the sun. The scales are on cardboard, newspapers, or paper, because they interact more consistently for this type of procedure.

Sixth step (storage): After drying, the scales must be slightly wet, because it is important that they stay in this state to acquire a flexible characteristic and adapt them to the different forms of handicraft products. In order not to give fungus, or attract some rodent, put naphthalene. They are stored in cardboard boxes, because if you use glass or plastic they get very dry, therefore losing quality.

After these procedures the fish scale is suitable for the use of handicraft.

4.5TYPES OF PRODUCTS MARKETED

Products made from scales are: Arrangements, necklaces, tiaras, earrings and bracelets, each one with its particularities in necessary inputs and processing time, and that also counts with the different skills of the artisans in execution.

There are some products that do not need to be dyed, because the "natural" color enhances the handmade work and shows the authentic side of the product. But for some, the scales are dyed in order to follow the trends of colors that are more in evidence, making them with a sophisticated design, modern reaching a greater number of interested customers, without leaving aside all its handmade essence.

Image 2 shows the scales in full condition to be used without dyeing.

Image 3 Scales ready.

Source: Own authorship (2016).

The dyeing process is made from the use of aniline gaucho, which is a dye dissolved in water and that for each liter of water one spoon of this product. After the paint is prepared, the scales are placed in the container and submerged for about 12 (twelve) hours, which is the time necessary for the complete dyeing. At the end of this process, they are strained to reuse the paint, which will return to the process of painting other scales, but with the color a little lighter than the first scales dyed. After painting, there is a wash, because the excess of paint can cause stains on the clothes of the users. In the Image it is possible to observe dyed scales ready to be used in the process.

Image 4 recycled5.

Source: Own authorship (2016).

The 4shot shows some arrangements produced with the dyed scales and others with the "natural" color, where the differences between them are displayed, in order to achieve the customers' requirements.

Image 6 -Errangements made from recycled fish scales.

Source: Own authorship (2016).

The products that come from the scales recycling process demonstrate an enormous authenticity, serving as a great influence in the search for customers. For *marketing* there are several possibilities to promote these products, as samples of them in events, projects focused on schools and universities, causing new audiences and new levels to be reached.

4.6 MANUFACTURING COSTS AND SELLING PRICES

The costs necessary to manufacture the parts are high because, as there is no great demand for the products, the necessary inputs are not bought on a large scale, so it has little bargaining power with suppliers, making it difficult to make the prices affordable. The time to produce a piece will depend on the skill of the craftswoman and also on the type of product, because the complexity of one piece to another is variable. But the average is one hour.

Each product is made according to the market trend and also with orders placed, but they are returned to work with the pulled production. With the expenses of the raw material for the elaboration of the manufactured products, an average cost of each product was obtained and the selling price of this handicraft, shown in table 1:

Table 1 - Gains per product.

Products	Cost of manufacture (R$)	Price of products sold (R$)
Arrangements	From 1.00 to 3.00	5,00
Necklaces	7,00	15,00
Tiara	6,00à 7,00	15,00
Earrings	5,00	10,00
Bracelets	3,00à 7,00	5,00 à 15,00

Source: Own authorship (2015).

This sales price also includes the labor of the associates. The income collected by these sales, part is divided between the members and another part is in the association itself specifically for the purchase of raw materials necessary for the production of new products, as well as for the dissemination of their craft project, through posters and samples at cultural fairs.

It is noticeable that the profit obtained from the sale of these products is small, because it is noticeable that with the raw material needed for the products and the labor of the craftswomen the cost rises, thus reducing the gain.

In view of this, it is important to reuse all inputs, inserting them all in the process or in new ways of not wasting them, so that they decrease costs further and increase profits. Besides improving the cooperative's financial performance, the use of all raw materials enables more opportunities for new members to be inserted.

4.7 USE OF FISH AND SCALE

The waste of raw material that is thrown to the environment is very much on the part of COPESCA, as no solution can be found to this serious problem. Of all the fish, only one part is used for the production of filet, and a small amount of scales that are recycled, the other parts, such as the viscera and the whole carcass, are not used.

All these inputs that are not used in the processes allow the fishing colony many options for reuse and consequently decrease the rejects, costs and increase profits. O desafio para isso é encontrar soluções inteligente e que não necessitem de grandes investimentos, pois a colônia não consegue arcar com altos custos.

Graph 1 shows the percentage of fish that the cooperative receives per week and how much is wasted and thrown to the environment:

Chart 1 -Relationship between utility and waste of fish.

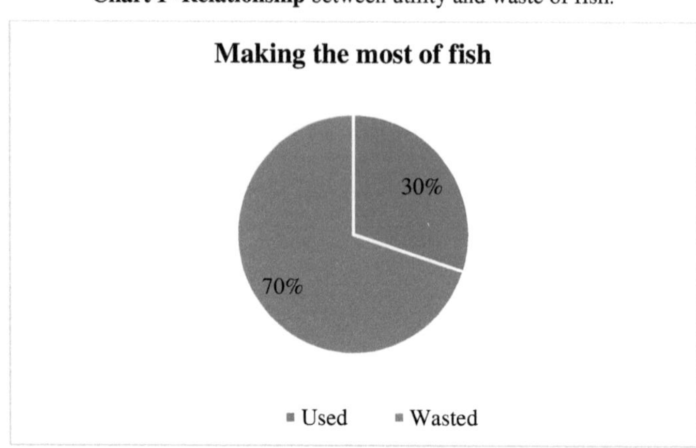

Source: Own authorship (2016).

About seventy percent of the fish is wasted, that includes the head, skin, viscera and the entire spinal structure and only the thirty percent is processed into filet to sell. The amount of fish that reaches the cooperative is around one thousand kilos per week, generating a waste of seven hundred kilos, which are thrown away and in addition to generating a high cost, contributes to the degradation of the environment.

The scales that are used in craftsmanship are also included in these scraps, Chart 2 shows the relationship between what is used and what is not.

According to the president of the cooperative, the quantity of scales that are removed from the fish is around eighty kilos and of these, only two and a half kilos are used to make the artisanal products. Chart 2 details this in more detail:

Chart 2 -Profitting from scales.

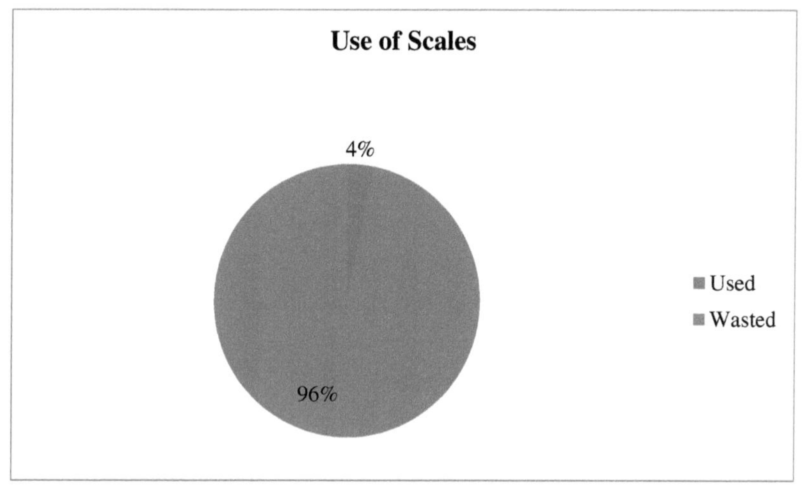

Source: Own authorship (2016).

More than ninety-six percent of the scales are not used, which could be of great potential to leverage production. However, the manpower is still not enough to reduce this percentage, the amount of inputs is very large, because the material is very "light" which entails a huge amount.

4.8 RECOMMENDATIONS

There are countless ways of reusing inputs that are not usable, in which we can highlight: most scales, the head, skin, viscera and spinal structure. They can be recycled in different ways, which will be presented later.

Most of the scales are not inserted in the craft process to be transformed into products and can be a great opportunity to increase the whole production. But for that, it would be necessary to participate too much in this system, through invitations or selection of people who would like to participate. Besides increasing the workplace, the amount of new inputs, new work tools and preparatory courses for new members, among others.

The skin can be used and transformed into other handcrafted products, as well as scales, but with new processes, new inputs, and with the need to take courses related to the new model of products, in order to offer more knowledge to make more ecological products and with a better quality in craftsmanship, besides being a way to motivate women who are being inserted in the Colony. And as there is the fish filleting process in COPESCA, necessary for the fillet production, it is easier to acquire the raw material (skin) in better conditions for use.

The spinal structure of the fish, the viscera and the head can be used in an intelligent way and that each day is gaining more strength in the national scenario, is the production of fish meal from the carcass. The nutritional value that the bones bring are many and serve as food for other animals or for the fish of the Colony, thus decreasing the cost in necessary ration for the meals, but can also serve as food composition of human beings, increasing the revenue of the organization.

In view of this, COPESCA will have a superior use in relation to the inputs that are currently recycled. This will be of paramount importance, as it will eliminate much of the waste by increasing its profits.

5 FINAL CONSIDERATIONS

This work aimed to demonstrate how social entrepreneurship through reverse logistics with a focus on sustainability contributes to the fishing colony - "COPESCA" in the municipality of Camalaú-PB.

At first, we studied the entire bibliography on the concepts and objectives of social entrepreneurship, which is an area in which we seek, through a sense of leadership and innovation well qualified, to insert people to a particular project that is concerned with benefiting all the people involved and their organization. Then, it was analyzed all the concepts of reverse logistics, which is an area focused on the reuse of inputs from procedures that from them, can take advantage of these waste and insert in new ways that help in the process of environmental conservation. For this reason, the whole set of content related to sustainability was also approached and studied, which is focused on a set of actions that seek to manage resources/services well in order to satisfy human needs and contribute to the maintenance of environmental resources and not spoil them.

Then, the significant importance of social entrepreneurship for the colony was shown, since when President Maria de Fátima innovated in a new process of shredding the fish "traíra" and received the gold award from SEBRAE businesswoman in the category rural producer in 2013 at state level and, later national and then with the initiative of inserting a group of women dedicated to crafts with scales, which made them generate unique opportunities for women who did not have in the community, but who were now included in a project in which they benefited, their families, and the colony also with all this social and sustainable approach.

In the interview with the president, it was noted how much the colony is concerned with investing its actions in social areas and even passing on the knowledge acquired to other municipalities, thus providing a better quality of life for other families through the marketing of these recycled products.

Soon after, analyses were made according to the triad of sustainability, where all the positive points in environmental, social and economic terms were shown. Where, it was perceived that the environment will improve with the removal of these wastes, because it will make possible a conservation of the whole area where the fishermen act, improving the vision of the place, decreasing the presence of insects and mainly reducing the emission of garbage thrown in the environment. In the social sphere this project has great value, because the members improve their quality of life and that of their families, because now they can feel more comfortable with their lives, once they begin to reach levels that before did not go through their heads, giving them pride and motivation for other women who find themselves in the same situation. And in the economic factor, it is important because this extra income offers the opportunity to meet needs that without this help would not be possible.

Sustainable perspectives of the colony in the three dimensions of the triad were also analyzed. In the economic area, the reduction of raw material costs, the increase in sales, partnerships with suppliers of the necessary inputs for production and a marketing focused on sustainability and the acquisition of new equipment were sought. In the environmental dimension, it sought to follow the standard of waste control, increase the recycling of inputs, raise awareness among fishermen, storage of inputs in specific containers and improve the entire area of operation of fishermen. And in the social dimension, to accompany and guide the members, to encourage members in sustainable practices, to insert more people into the cooperative and be a reference for the community and region.

In the process of recycling the scales coming from the fish, the necessary steps for the process were addressed: the collection, which is done by the associates themselves and that from the associates of the colony that fish and do the cleaning of the fish, delivering the scales to the women; then is the washing, which starts with the division of the types of scales to start with the washing that is only with water; hygienization, the scales are submerged in buckets that contain water mixed with sanitary water to make a more specific cleaning and that later are removed and washed again in running water; in bleaching, the scales are deposited in containers containing a bleach without the chlorine, leaving them soft and smelly; in drying, which occurs in a covered place, without exposure to the sun; and the last step of the scales recycling process is storage, which is done in cardboard boxes.

The products in which the scales were part of the process were shown, which are, arrangements, necklaces, tiaras, earrings and bracelets. And that some of them are dyed and others are not, in order to reach as many customers as possible. We also analyzed the costs that the associates were based on to manufacture and insert the sales price. According to them: the arrangements had a manufacturing cost of one (1) to three (3) reais and were sold for five (5) reais; the necklaces, a cost of seven (7) reais and sold for fifteen (15) reais; tiaras, manufactured at 6.00 (six) to 7.00 (seven) and sold for 15.00 (fifteen); earrings, cost 5.00 (five) and sold for 10.00 (ten); bracelets, cost 3.00 (three) to 7.00 (seven) and sold for a range 5.00 (five) to 15.00 (fifteen).

It was also analyzed how much all the inputs were used and how much wasted in the environment. The figures showed that the waste is very large, about seventy percent of the fish is wasted and only the other thirty percent that are somehow used. And the scales are even more serious, because more than ninety-six percent of them are not used, leaving four percent in the hands of the associates for the recycling process.

So the contributions of social entrepreneurship with the help of reverse logistics by sustainable means are exorbitant, because several people, several families have benefited both in social and economic aspects and also in environmental actions to care for the ecosystem. COPESCA has also placed itself at a level that can become a great reference in the region for using such acts to improve the life of an entire community.

Therefore, according to the results achieved, it can be stated that all objectives that were included in this survey were achieved.

The limitation was the data collection period, which was from June to October 2015, causing small variations in information for the current days.

As proposals for future work, a more specific study of all costs relating to the recycling process and a more detailed analysis of the use of all raw materials are recommended.

REFERENCES

BALLOU, R. H. **Supply Chain Management / Business Logistics** - 5th edition. Porto Alegre: Bookman Editora, 2006.

BARBOSA, José. **Fish farming as an investment alternative for rural producers in the Middle Amazon Region**. Fortaleza, 1992. 150 p. Dissertation (Masters in Rural Economics), UFCE, 1992.

BOGDAN, R. S.; BIKEN, S. **Qualitative research in education**: an introduction to theory and methods. 12.ed. Porto: Porto, 2003.

BRINCKERHOFF, Peter C. Social entrepreneurship – the art of mission-based venture development. New York: Wiley, 2000.

BRUNDTLAND, G. H. (Org.) **Our common future**. Rio de Janeiro: FGV, 1987.
CAMINO V., Ronnie de.; MÜLLER, Sabine. **Sustainability of agriculture and natural resources**: bases for establishing indicators. San José: IICA, 1993.

CANEPA, Carla. **Sustainable Cities:** the municipality as a locus of sustainability. São Paulo: RCS Publisher, 2007.

CHAVES, G. BATALHA, M. **Do consumers value the collection of recyclable packaging? A case study of reverse logistics in a network of hypermarkets**. Federal University of São Carlos. São Carlos, 2006.

COLLIS, Jill; HUSSEY, Roger. **Research in administration:** a practical guide for undergraduate and graduate students. 2. ed. Porto Alegre: Bookman, 2005.
DEMO, Pedro. **Research and knowledge building**. Rio de Janeiro: Brazilian Time, 1996.

DOLABELA, F. The rope and the dream. **HSM Management Magazine**, 2010, 80, pp. 128-132.

DORNELAS, J. C. A. **Entrepreneurship**: turning ideas into business. 3. ed. Rio de Janeiro: Elsevier, 2008.

FAO. **Codeofconduct for responsiblefisheries**. Rome, 1995.41 p.

FOUCAULT, M. **The order of speech**. São Paulo: Loyola Editions, 2002.

FREIRE, A. J. M. **Study of generation and disposal of solid waste from a cash &carry.** - Salvador, 2010. Monograph (undergraduate) - Faculdade de Tecnologia SENAI Cimatec, 2010.

GIL, A.C. How to develop research projects. 3. ed. São Paulo: Atlas, 1991.

GIL, A. C. **How to Elaborate Research Projects.** 5.ed. São Paulo: Atlas, 2010.

HONG, YuhChing. **Inventory management in the Integrated Logistics chain.** São Paulo: Atlas. 1999.

IRIGARAY H.A., VIANNA A., NASSER J.E., et al., **Product and Brand Development Management.** 2nd ed, Rio de Janeiro, Ed FGV, 2006.

JONGEWARD, C. Sustainable livelihoods within global market places: rural artisans in Thailand. **Women & Environments International Magazine,** Spring2002, Issue 54/55.

KAZAZIAN, Thierry (Org.). **There will be the Age of Light Things**: design and sustainable development. São Paulo: SENAC, 2005.

KOTLER P., KELLER K. **Marketing Management,** 12 edition, São Paulo: Pearson Prentine Hall, 2006.

KOTLER, P.; ARMSTRONG, G. **Marketing principles.** 9. ed. São Paulo: Prentice Hall, 2003.

LACERDA, L. **Reverse Logistics, a vision of basic concepts and operational practices.** Center for Logistics Studies - COPPEAD - UFRJ - 2009.Available at:<http://www.ilos.com.br/site/index.php?option=com_contentask=viewd=763temid=74>. Accessed on: 20/05/2010.

LAMB JR., C. W.; HAIR JR., J. F.; McDANIEl, C. **Marketing principles.** São Paulo: Thompson, 2004.

LEITE, P. R. **Reverse Logistics** - environment and competitiveness. São Paulo: Prentice Hall, 2003.

MELO NETO, Francisco de Paula de. FROES, César. **Social entrepreneurship** - the transition to a sustainable society. Rio de Janeiro: Qualitymark, 2002.

MILANI, Carlos. **Environmental policy instruments. New NAEA booklets,** v. 1, n. 1, p. 79-109, June 1999.

MINAYO, Maria Cecília de Souza. **The Challenge of Knowledge.** São Paulo: Hucitec, 1993.

NASSER, J. Monir. **Development Communities.** Avia Internacional, 2002.

NOVAES, A. G. **Logistics and Distribution Chain Management**. 3. ed. Rio de Janeiro January: Elsevier, 2.007.

OLIVEIRA, Edson Marques. **Social entrepreneurship in Brazil:** foundations and strategies. 2004. Thesis (Doctorate)- Universidade Estadual Paulista - Unesp, Franca, 2004.

OSTRENSKY, A; BOEGER W. **Piscicultura:** Fundamentos e técnicas de manejo, Agropecuária, 1998, 211p.

PEREIRA NETO J. T.; **Composting manual:** low cost process. UFV. 2007.
National basic sanitation survey 2008. Rio de Janeiro: IBGE, 2010. 218 p.
It comes with 1 CD-ROM. Available at: <http://www.ibge.gov.br/home/estatistica/ population/continent of life/pnsb2008/PNSB_2008.pdf>. Access in: Jun. 2011.

RODRIGUEZ, J. M. M. **Sustainable development: conceptual levels and models**. In: RODRIGUEZ, J. M. M; SILVA, E. V. da. Local sustainable development. Fortaleza: Federal University of Ceará, 2001.

SANTOS, J. S.; BARBOSA, R. F.; CARVALHO, E. N. **The Use of Reverse Logistics in Solid Waste Management.** CDSA/ UFCG, 2013.

SEVERINO, Antônio Joaquim. **Methodology of scientific work**. - – 23. Ed. Ver. And current. - São Paulo: Cortez, 2007.

SILVA, E. L.; MENEZES, E. M. **Methodology of research and elaboration of dissertation-** 3. ed. rev. actual. - Florianópolis: UFSC Distance Learning Laboratory, 2001. 121p.

SILVA, Barbara Cravo da. **Initiatives for the development of sustainable fashion**. In: ANUAL SCIENTIFIC INITIATION MEETING, 18., 2009, Londrina. Annals... Londrina: UEL, 2009. p. 12.

SOTO, A. S. Lasartesanias and design. In: NOVELO, V. (coord.) **La capacitación de artesanosen México, una revisión.** Mexico City: Plaza y Valdes, 2003.

TRIVIÑOS, A. N. S. **Introduction to social science research**: qualitative research in education. São Paulo: Atlas, 1987.

VALE, G. M. V. **Collective Entrepreneurs in Organizational Networks** - New Agents Generating a Differentiated Standard of Competitiveness. WorkPaper. In: Proceedings of the XXVIII National Meeting of Graduate Programs in Administration, Curitiba, 2004.

VALENTI, Wagner Cotroni et al. **Aquaculture in Brazil**: Basis for Sustainable Development. Brasília: CNPq, 2000. 399 p.

VERGARA, Sylvia Constant. **Management research projects and reports**. 3. ed. São Paulo: Atlas, 2000.

YIN, R. K. **Case study**: planning and methods. 2.ed. Porto Alegre:Bookman, 2001.

ZIKMUND, W. G. **Business research methods**.5.ed. Fort Worth, TX: Dryden, 2000.

Printed by Books on Demand GmbH, Norderstedt / Germany